Science That's Appropriate an

This science resource book was written with two goals in mind:

- to provide "good" science for your students
- to make it easy for you

What makes this book "good" science?

When you follow the step-by-step lessons in this book, you'll be using an instructional model that makes science education relevant to real life.

- Your students will be drawn in by interesting activities that encourage them to express what they already know about a concept.

- Your students will participate in hands-on discovery experiences and be guided to describe the experiences in their own words. Together, you'll record the experiences in both class and individual logbooks.

- You'll provide explanations and vocabulary that will help your students accurately explain what they have experienced.

- Your students will have opportunities to apply their new understandings to new situations.

What makes this book easy for you?

- The step-by-step activities are easy to understand and have illustrations where it's important.

- The resources you need are at your fingertips — record sheets; logbook forms; and other reproducibles such as minibooks, task cards, picture cards, and pages to make into overhead transparencies.

- Each science concept is presented in a self-contained section. You can decide to do the entire book or pick only those sections that enhance your own curriculum.

> For sites on the World Wide Web that supplement the material in this resource book, go to http://www.evan-moor.com and look for the Product Updates link on the main page.

Using Logbooks as Learning Tools

Logbooks are valuable learning tools for several reasons:
- Logbooks give students an opportunity to put what they are learning into their own words.
- Putting ideas into words is an important step in internalizing new information. Whether spoken or written, this experience allows students to synthesize their thinking.
- Explaining and describing experiences help students make connections between several concepts and ideas.
- Logbook entries allow the teacher to catch misunderstandings right away and then reteach.
- Logbooks are a useful reference for students and a record of what has been learned.

Two Types of Logbooks

The Class Logbook

A class logbook is completed by the teacher and the class together. The teacher records student experiences and helps students make sense of their observations. The class logbook is a working document. You will return to it often for a review of what has been learned. As new information is acquired, make additions and corrections to the logbook.

Individual Science Logbooks

Individual students process their own understanding of investigations by writing their own responses in their own logbooks. Two types of logbook pages are provided in this unit.

1. Open-ended logbook pages:
   Pages 4 and 5 provide two choices of pages that can be used to respond to activities in the unit. At times you may wish students to write in their own logbooks and then share their ideas as the class logbook entry is made. After the class logbook has been completed, allow students to revise and add information to their own logbooks. At other times you may wish students to copy the class logbook entry into their own logbooks.

2. Specific logbook pages:
   You will find record forms or activity sheets following many activities that can be added to each student's logbook.

At the conclusion of the unit, reproduce a copy of the logbook cover on page 3 for each student. Students can then organize both types of pages and staple them with the cover.

   Water • EMC 862

_____'s
Name

Water Log

Name _____

This is what I learned about water today:

Note: Reproduce this form for students to record science investigations for their individual logs.

Name ______________________________

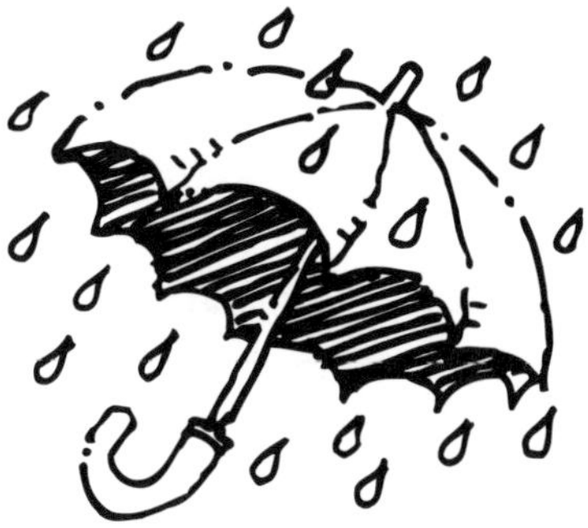

Investigation ______________________________

____

What we did:

____

____

____

What we saw:

____

____

____

What we learned:

____

____

____

Water is a liquid. It has certain properties.

Describe Water

- Give each student a paper cup containing water. (Use bottled water to eliminate the possibility of odor and taste.) Explain that you don't want them to guess what is in the cup yet. They are to listen and follow your directions.

   Have students look in their cups and describe the contents. *(It looks shiny. It doesn't have any color. It is clear.)*
   Have them smell the contents. *(It doesn't have a smell.)*
   Have them stick a finger in the contents. *(It feels wet.)*
   Have them taste the contents. Say "Now name what is in your cup."

- Begin a class water log. Ask students to tell the ways they know something is water. List their observations about water on a chart entitled "Water." Use the students' own descriptions. Changes will be made as vocabulary and knowledge increases.

- Ask if anyone knows a name for things that look and move like water. If no one responds with "liquid," provide the term for your students. Then ask them to name other liquids they know.

Water

It doesn't have a color.

It doesn't smell.

It is wet.

Water Investigations

The three investigations described on pages 7 and 8 will help students discover these properties of water:

1. Water takes the shape of any container.
2. Water flows downhill.
3. Water has surface tension.

Rotate small groups of students through all three centers before doing the follow-up activities.

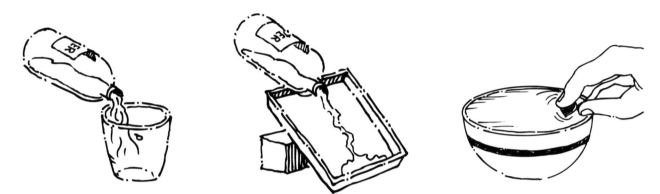

Preparation

1. Place the materials for each investigation in a center.
2. Reproduce the direction charts on pages 10–12. Post each chart with the correct center.
3. Read center charts with students. Answer any questions about procedures.
4. Explain cleanup procedures.

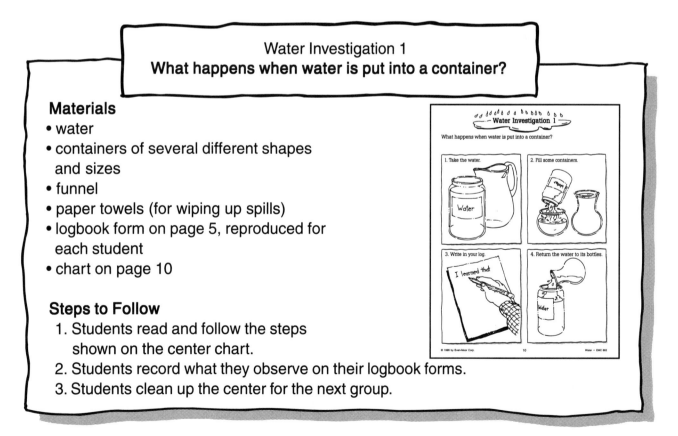

Water Investigation 1
What happens when water is put into a container?

Materials
- water
- containers of several different shapes and sizes
- funnel
- paper towels (for wiping up spills)
- logbook form on page 5, reproduced for each student
- chart on page 10

Steps to Follow
1. Students read and follow the steps shown on the center chart.
2. Students record what they observe on their logbook forms.
3. Students clean up the center for the next group.

Water Investigation 2
What happens when water is poured onto a slanting surface?

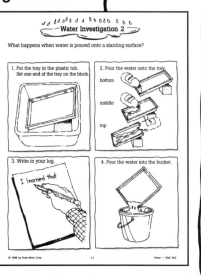

Materials

- bottle of water
- tray
- wooden block
- plastic tub
- bucket
- logbook form on page 5, reproduced for each student
- chart on page 11

Steps to Follow

1. Students read and follow the steps shown on the center chart.
2. Students record what they observe on their logbook forms.
3. Students empty any water on the tray or in the tub into the bucket and wipe up any spills.

Water Investigation 3
Can you fill a bowl with water above the brim?

Materials

- bowl
- water
- pennies
- record sheet on page 13, reproduced for each student
- chart on page 12

Steps to Follow

Have students work in pairs. Each partner takes a turn putting pennies in the bowl and counting the number of pennies used by his/her partner.

1. Students fill their bowls all the way to the top.
2. Slowly slide the pennies into the water one at a time. Watch what happens to the surface of the water as the pennies are put into the bowl.
3. Carefully count how many pennies go into the bowl before the water spills over.
4. Students record results on their record sheets.

Follow Up

- After everyone has had a chance to do the investigations, facilitate a class discussion of the properties of water. Add this new information to the class logbook.

    "What did you see when you put water into the different containers?" (Water poured. Water filled the shape of the containers.)

    "What happened when you poured water on different parts of the tray?" (Water went down to the bottom of the tray. The water moved fast.)

    "What happened as you put pennies into the bowl?" (The water raised up a little bit above the top of the bowl.)

    Explain that this happens because water has a property called surface tension which holds the water together until a breaking point is reached.

    "What happened when you put too many pennies in the bowl?" (The water spilled out of the bowl.)

- Review what students learned from their exploration of liquids. Then read *Water and Other Liquids* by Robert Mebane (Twenty-First Century Books, 1995) or *A Drop of Water: A Book of Science Wonder* by Walter Wick (Scholastic, 1995) for further information about the properties of liquids.

- Make corrections and additions to the class log. *(Water takes the shape of a container. Water flows downhill. Water has surface tension.)* Explain that the things listed to describe water are called properties of water.

Assess Understanding

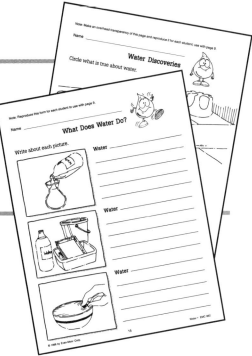

- Make an overhead transparency of page 14. Reproduce a copy of the page for each student. Complete the page together.

- Reproduce page 15 for each student. Students write about the properties of water illustrated.

Extension Activity — Mixing Liquids

Explore further to discover what happens when water is mixed with other liquids. Reproduce page 16 for each student. Call on several students to assist with the demonstration.

Materials

- water
- fruit juice
- vegetable oil (add a few drops of food coloring)
- measuring cup
- two clear plastic containers labeled 1 and 2 with secure lids
- record sheet on page 16, reproduced for each student

Steps to Follow

1. Select students to fill jar 1 with equal amounts of water and fruit juice.
2. Select students to fill jar 2 with equal amounts of oil and water.
3. Select students to shake the jars briskly. All students observe the jars for a few minutes.
4. Students record what happens on their record sheets.

Conclude the lesson by asking "What did you see when you mixed water with other liquids?" *(Water mixed with the juice. It didn't mix with the oil.)*

What happens when water is put into a container?

1. Take the water.

2. Fill some containers.

3. Write in your log.

I learned that

4. Return the water to its bottles.

Water • EMC 862

Water Investigation 2

What happens when water is poured onto a slanting surface?

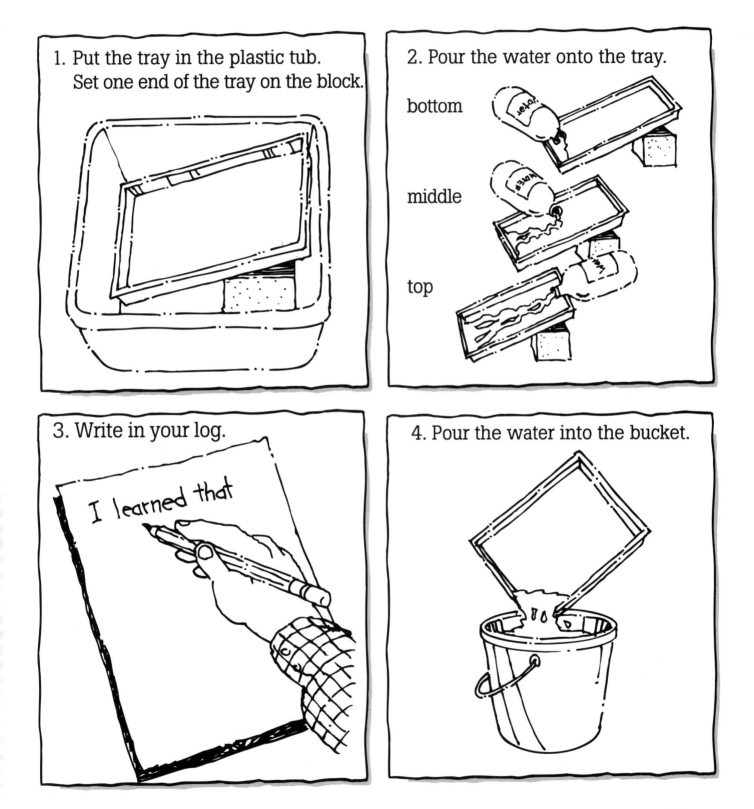

1. Put the tray in the plastic tub.
   Set one end of the tray on the block.

2. Pour the water onto the tray.

bottom

middle

top

3. Write in your log.

I learned that

4. Pour the water into the bucket.

Can you fill a bowl with water above the brim?

1. Put water in the bowl.
   Fill it to the top.

2. Color to show water in the first bowl on your record sheet.

3. Slowly put pennies into the bowl one at a time.

4. Count the pennies.

5. Stop when the water spills over.

6. Finish your record sheet.

Water • EMC 862

Note: Reproduce this form for each student to use with page 8.

Name _____

How Many Pennies Did It Take?

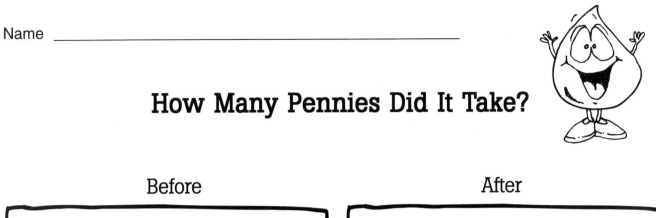

Before   After

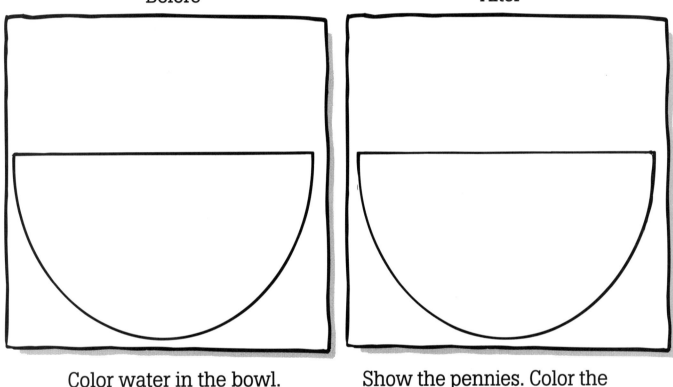

Color water in the bowl.   Show the pennies. Color the
water to show what happened.

I discovered that _____

_____

_____

_____

     13   Water • EMC 862

Note: Make an overhead transparency of this page and reproduce it for each student; use with page 9.

Name _____

Water Discoveries

Circle what is true about water.

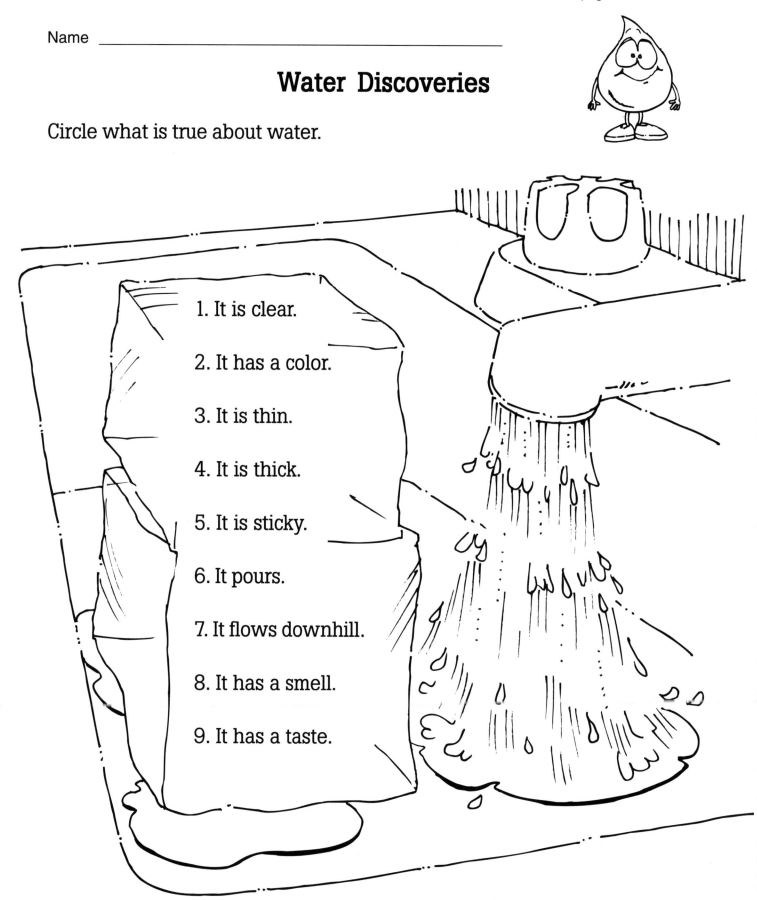

1. It is clear.

2. It has a color.

3. It is thin.

4. It is thick.

5. It is sticky.

6. It pours.

7. It flows downhill.

8. It has a smell.

9. It has a taste.

Water • EMC 862

Name _____

What Does Water Do?

Write about each picture.

Water _____

_____

_____

_____

_____

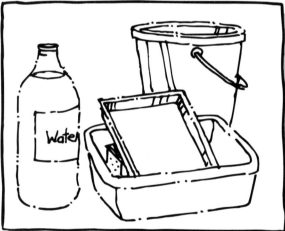

Water _____

_____

_____

_____

_____

Water _____

_____

_____

_____

_____

Water • EMC 862

Name _____

Do All Liquids Mix?

Draw and color the liquids to show what happened.

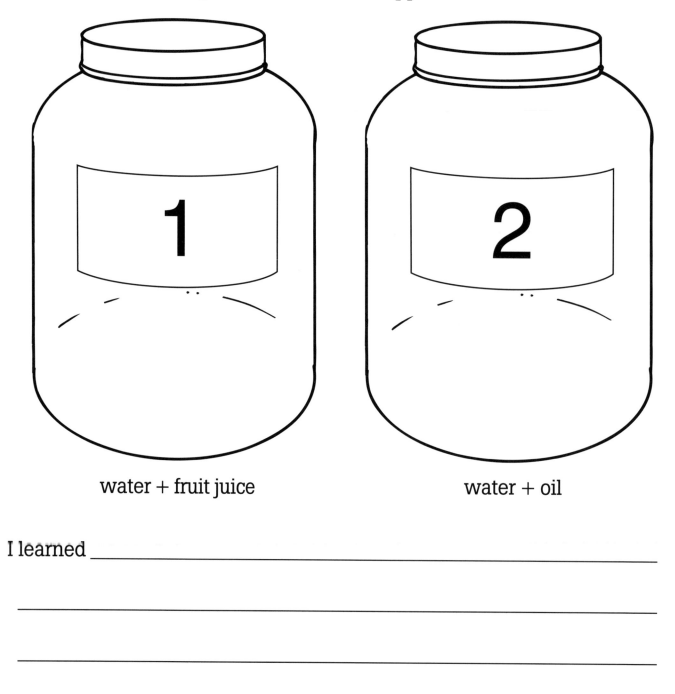

water + fruit juice   water + oil

I learned _____

_____

_____

_____

Water occurs in three forms in nature – liquid, solid, gas.

Find the Water

- Check your district audiovisual catalog for appropriate videos on the forms of water.

- Make your own video showing water forms in ways directly related to daily life (liquid water – flowing from faucet, in bathtub, sprinkling lawn; gas – water vapor from boiling teakettle, foggy shower; ice – ice cubes in glass).

  Show the video to your students. Prompt them to watch closely to find all the places water is shown.

  After seeing the video, ask students to describe what they have discovered about the forms of water. Record this in the class water log on a page entitled "3 Forms of Water."

- Reproduce copies of page 20 for each student. Have the students find and mark water in various forms.

Solid, Liquid, Gas

- Introduce the proper names for the three forms of water (water – liquid; ice – solid; water vapor or steam – gas). Add these to the class log.

- Reproduce page 21 for each student. They are to name the pictures and fill in the missing words.

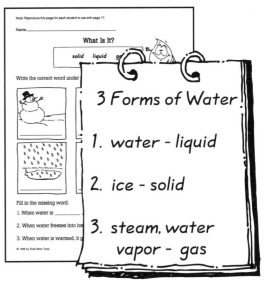

A Water Shape Book

Students make a shape book to tell what they know about the three forms of water.

1. Reproduce pages 22–25 for each student.
2. Students cut out the pages and staple them together at the top.
3. Students complete each page.

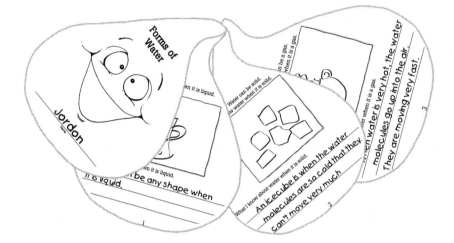

Extension Activities — Forms of Water

Water Is the Only One

Explain that water is the only substance that can be found in all three forms — liquid, solid, and gas — in nature.

Ask students to name other liquids they know. List these on the chalkboard.

Ask "Have you ever seen solid *(gasoline)*?" Students might say yes for fruit juice since they eat frozen juice bars. Remind students that frozen juice bars are made by people. They are not a part of nature.

Water • EMC 862

Solid — Liquid — Gas

• Some students will be ready for a simple explanation of matter. Make an overhead transparency of page 26. Share as much of the following information as is appropriate with your students.

Everything is made up of tiny pieces called atoms. Atoms are so tiny, they can't be seen even with a microscope. Atoms of different kinds sometimes join together. Two kinds — oxygen and hydrogen — come together to make water molecules.

Frozen water molecules are attracted to one another and stay close together. When water molecules freeze, they don't move around very much.

When water molecules are a liquid, they move around but stay fairly close together. This is why they take on the shape of any container.

When water molecules get hot, they move faster and farther apart. Some of the molecules escape into the air as gas.

• Select students to act the part of each type of water.

Solid - Students stand close together, then move very slowly, staying together.
Liquid - Students stand farther apart, then move in and around each other.
Gas - Students stand far apart, then move about quickly.

solid   liquid   gas

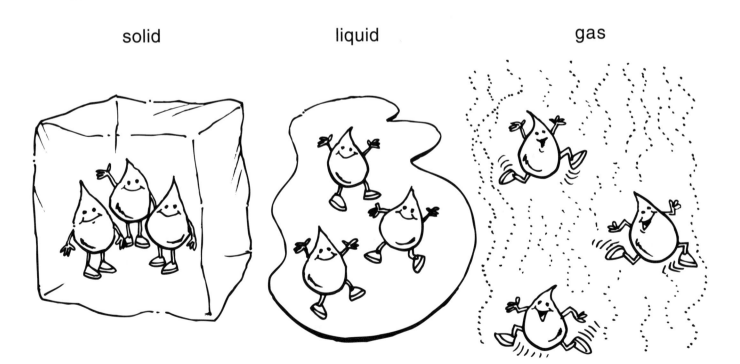

Find the Water

Water • EMC 862

Name_____

What Is It?

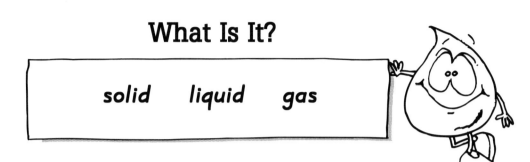

solid   liquid   gas

Write the correct word under each picture.

Fill in the missing word.

1. When water is _____ , we can drink it, wash with it, or swim in it.

2. When water freezes into ice or snow, it is _____ .

3. When water is warmed, it goes into the air as a _____ .

         Water • EMC 862

Note: Reproduce this shape book for each student to use with page 18.

Forms of
Water

_____
Name

Water • EMC 862

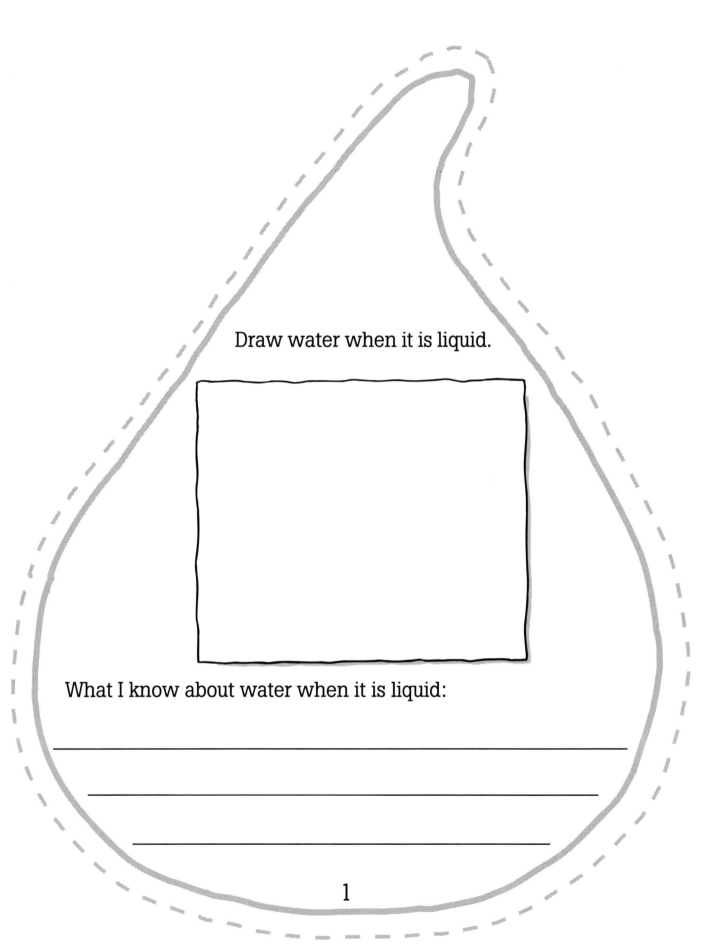

Draw water when it is liquid.

What I know about water when it is liquid:

_____

_____

_____

1

Water • EMC 862

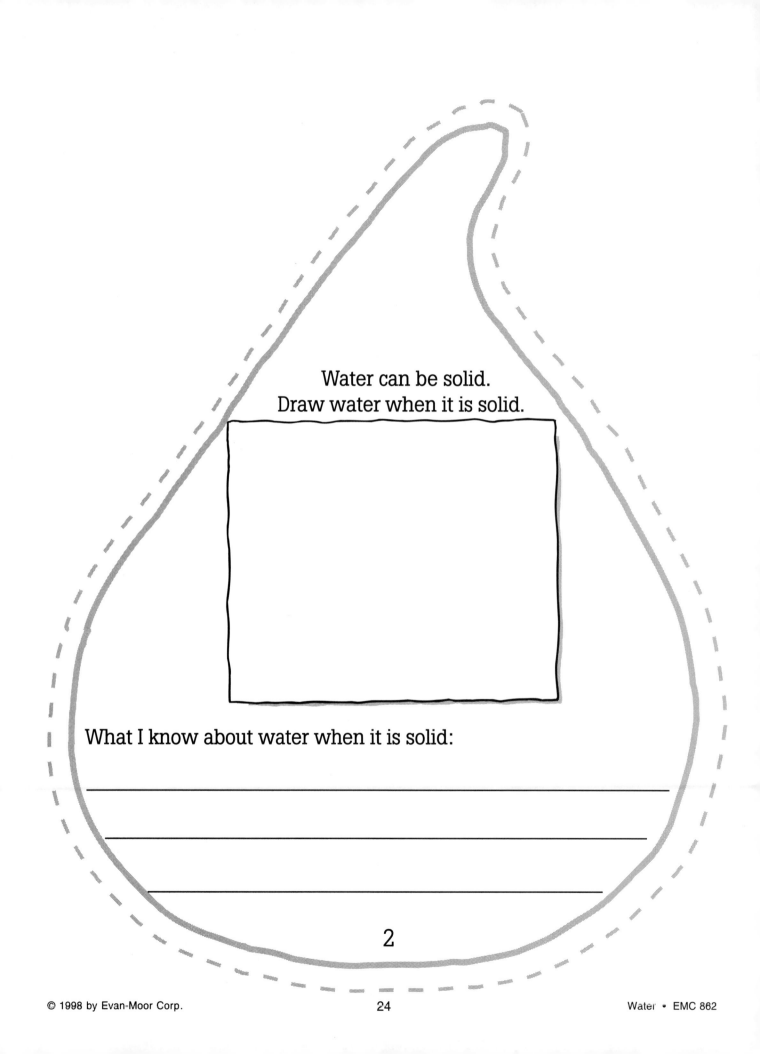

Water can be solid.
Draw water when it is solid.

What I know about water when it is solid:

_____

_____

_____

2

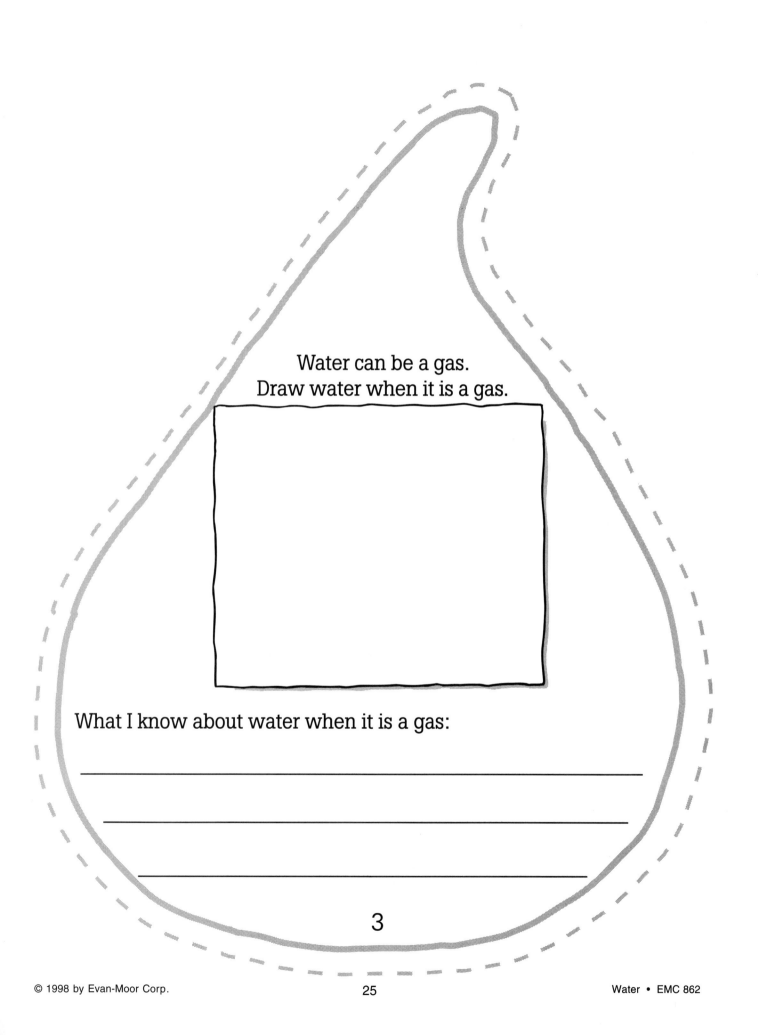

Water can be a gas.
Draw water when it is a gas.

What I know about water when it is a gas:

_____

_____

_____

3

Water • EMC 862

Solid

Liquid

Gas

Cold changes water from a liquid to a solid.

Water Expands When It Freezes

Divide the class into small groups to investigate the formation of ice and its properties.

Materials

- water
- plastic glasses
- permanent marking pens
- access to a freezer
- logbook form on page 5, reproduced for each student

Steps to Follow

1. Students fill their glasses 2/3 full and draw a line to mark the water level.
2. The glass is set in a freezer and left for several hours.
3. Students retrieve the glass and mark the level of the ice.
4. They write their observations in their individual logs.

Follow Up

- Provide time for students to share what they discovered. Ask
  "What kind of change did you see? *(The water changed to ice.)*
  "What word do we use when water changes to ice?" *(Freezing)*
  "What is the other word we learned to call water?" *(Liquid)*
  Explain that objects like ice have a special name, too. They are called solids.
- Write a page for the class log entitled "Cold Changes Water." Have students write about the investigation for their individual logs using the form on page 5.

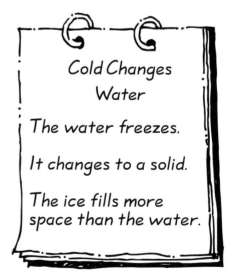

Cold Changes Water

The water freezes.

It changes to a solid.

The ice fills more space than the water.

Water • EMC 862

Does Ice Float?

Extend student understanding of the properties of water by doing this demonstration with student assistance.

Materials

- ice cube
- plastic glass
- water

Steps to Follow

Call on students to do the following steps as classmates observe:

1. Put an ice cube in the glass.
2. Fill the glass to the top with water.
3. Observe what happens to the ice cube. (It floats on top of the water.)
4. Push the ice cube down into the glass and let it go. (It pops back up to the surface.)
5. Ask:
   a. "What did the ice cube do when it was put in the water?" *(It floated.)*
   b. "What did the ice cube do when it was pushed down and then let go?"
      (It came back up to the surface.)
   c. "Is water lighter when it is a liquid or when it is solid?"

> Most things contract when they freeze. Water does the opposite. When ice freezes it expands and increases in volume. Therefore, the ice is lighter than the same volume of water.

Follow Up

- Reproduce the log form on page 5 for each student. Have students record what happened in the experiment.

- Reproduce page 31 for each student. They are to circle the facts that are true of water when it freezes. Read the statements aloud for beginning readers.

- Engage students in a discussion of how ice is helpful to people and how it might be harmful to people. Add their conclusions to the class log page entitled "Cold Changes Water" and in their individual logs.

What's the Temperature?

It is difficult in the confines of the classroom to accurately calculate the temperature at which ice freezes. However, you can explore the changes in temperature that occur when water is chilled.

Materials

- two bowls
- water
- a bag of crushed ice
- thermometer
- form on page 32, reproduced for each student
- ice tray

Steps to Follow

1. Leave the bag of ice out until 2/3 of it has melted.
2. Fill one bowl with room temperature water.
3. Place the thermometer in the water. Hold it there while students count to 60. Check the temperature.
4. Have everyone record the temperature on the record form by coloring the first thermometer. (Demonstrate this on an overhead transparency of page 32 if this is your students' first experience with thermometers.)
5. Fill the second bowl with the cold water and ice.
6. Place the thermometer in the icy water and have students count to 60. Check the thermometer.
7. Everyone records the temperature on the second thermometer on the record sheet.
8. Ask students to explain what has happened. *(You can measure how cold water gets. Water with ice in it is colder than water without ice.)* Have students use their prior knowledge to explain what makes water turn to ice. *(When water gets really cold, it freezes into ice.)* Fill a tray with water and put it in the freezer to verify that this is what happens.

Explain that when water reaches 32° F (0° C) it becomes the solid form that we call ice.

Extension Activity — Icebergs

Icebergs are the biggest examples of solid water in nature. Use the following activities to explore them with your students.

- Read *Danger – Iceberg!* by Roma Gans (Thomas Y. Crowell, 1987) or *Icebergs: Facts, Stories, Projects* by Jenny Wood (Puffin Books, 1990).

- Encourage students to share what they learned about icebergs from the story. Ask them to explain how an iceberg and an ice cube are alike. (*Both frozen water. Both float in water. Both melt.*)

- Reproduce page 33 for each student. Have them draw a picture of an iceberg floating in the ocean. Then write three facts they know about icebergs.

Name _____

When Water Freezes

Circle what happens to water when it freezes.

1. It becomes ice.

2. It turns blue.

3. It takes up more space.

4. It becomes a solid.

5. It gets salty.

6. It can float.

7. It gets smaller.

8. It can go up into the air.

Water • EMC 862

Note: Reproduce this page for each student to use with page 29.

Name _____

What's the Temperature?

Color the thermometer to show the temperature.

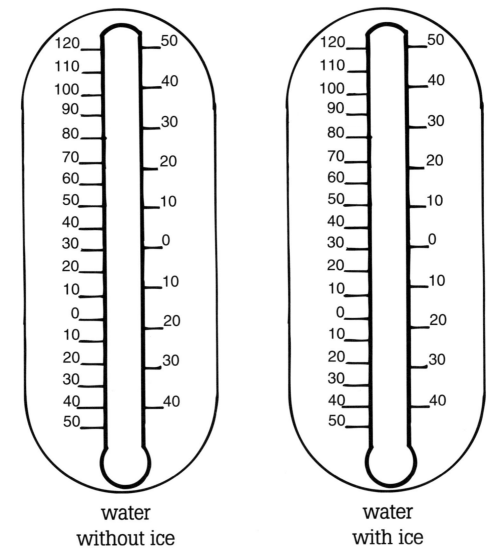

water
without ice

water
with ice

How is water with ice different than water without ice?

_____

What happens to water when it becomes very cold?

_____

Name _____

Iceberg

Draw an iceberg floating in the ocean.

Write three things you learned about icebergs.

1. _____

_____

2. _____

_____

3. _____

_____

Heat changes water from a liquid to a gas.

Mysterious Disappearing Water

Divide the class into small groups to investigate evaporation.

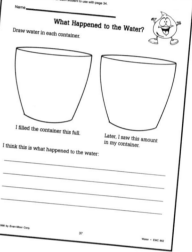

Materials

- clear plastic containers
- water
- permanent marking pens
- record form on page 37, reproduced for each student

Steps to Follow

1. Members of each group write their names along the bottom edge of their container.
2. One person in the group fills the container half full of water.
3. One person makes a mark to indicate the water level.
4. Place the container in a warm place such as a window sill.
5. After a few days have the groups collect their containers. See if students can explain what has occurred.
6. Students record what they have observed.

Follow Up

Record student discoveries on a page in the class log entitled "Water Can Change Its Form."

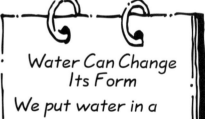

Water Can Change Its Form

We put water in a container.

We set the container on the window sill.

Some of the water disappeared.

We think the warm sun made this happen.

Boiling Water Evaporates

Explain that, while we can see the results of evaporation when we set water in a warm place, we don't actually see it happening. But by boiling water we can make water evaporate right before our eyes.

Materials

- pan
- water
- heat source
- masking tape

Steps to Follow

1. Tape off the area where water will be boiled. Students are to remain behind the line unless asked to assist the teacher.
2. Student fills the pan half full of water.
3. Heat the water to boiling as students watch. (Continue boiling long enough to show a reduction in the amount of water.)
4. Call on students to explain what they observe. You may need to ask questions to get the discussion started.
   "What kind of change did you see?" (*Steam came off the water.*)
   "What word do we use when water disappears into the air?" (If no one knows the term "evaporation," provide it.)
   "What is the other word we learned to call water?" *(Liquid)* "What did we learn to call ice?" *(Solid)*
   Explain that when water evaporates it becomes a gas. (You may need to clarify that this is not the gas used in a car. That "gas" is just a short way of saying gasoline.)

Follow Up

- With student help, rewrite the information in the class log. Have students write in their individual logs.

- Reproduce page 38 for each student. They are to mark the place in each picture where water has turned from a liquid to a gas.

- Since you measured the temperature at which water freezes, you may have students who want to know the temperature at which water boils. Use a candy thermometer to check this. When the water begins to boil, step outside the taped off area with the thermometer and ask a student to read the temperature.

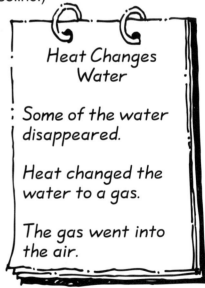

Heat Changes Water

Some of the water disappeared.

Heat changed the water to a gas.

The gas went into the air.

Water • EMC 862

Extension Activities — Evaporation

Evaporation Keeps Us Cool

Explore how evaporation can be helpful to us on a hot day.

1. Have students make folded paper fans.
2. Take the class outside to run around the playground until they feel hot and "sweaty."
3. Have everyone fan themselves with their paper fans. Ask "What happened when you fanned yourself?" "Why did you feel cooler?"

Explain that what has occurred is evaporation. Fanning helps to speed up the evaporation of the sweat. As the sweat evaporates, the body feels cooler.

Evaporation Makes Wet Things Dry

• Discuss how evaporation can be helpful on laundry day. Say "Some people hang their laundry outside to dry. Can you explain how the clothes get dry?" *(The hot sun evaporates the water in the clothes.)* Do the following activity to explore this concept.

1. Divide students into small groups. Give each group two pieces of cloth.
2. Each group dips their cloths in water and wrings them out. They place one in a sunny spot and the other in a shady spot.
3. Have them observe the cloths periodically.

Discuss what they observe. Ask "Where did the water go?" *(Into the air.)* "Which cloth dried the fastest?" *(The one in the sunlight.)* "Why do you think it dried the fastest?" *(Hotter temperatures cause faster evaporation.)*

• Reproduce the logbook form on page 4 for each student. Have them write about what they learned about evaporation. Place the form in their individual logs.

36

Name _____

What Happened to the Water?

Draw water in each container.

I filled the container this full.

Later, I saw this amount
in my container.

I think this is what happened to the water:

_____

_____

_____

_____

Name_____

Where's the Gas?

Put an X on each picture where water is turning to a gas.

 Water • EMC 862

Water can turn from a gas to a liquid.

Water from Air

Investigation 1

- Pass out small mirrors to students (or use classroom windows if it's a cold day). Have them breathe on the mirror several times, observing the change. Then have them rub the mirror and describe what they see and feel. Ask "What do you feel? Where did the water come from?" (*The water vapor in the child's warm breath condenses on the cooler mirror.*) List student ideas on the chalkboard. Do not provide the explanation at this time.

- Then divide the class into partners. Have each pair do the following experiment to observe the change from gas to water.

Materials

- two plastic glasses
- ice
- page 43, reproduced for each student
- paper towels (for cleanup)

Steps to Follow

1. Students set the glasses side-by-side.
2. They fill one of the glasses with ice and observe what happens.
3. Students record what they see.

Follow Up

- Have students share what they observed.
  "What happened to the glass with ice?"
  "What happened to the glass with no ice?"
  "Where did the water on the outside of the glass come from?"
  "Why didn't the empty glass get wet?"
  At this time you are listening to their interpretation. You will clarify any misinformation later.

- Record their observations in the class log on a page entitled "Gas to Liquid." Write about the experiment for individual logs using the form on page 5.

Gas to Liquid

The glass with ice got wet on the outside.

Some kids think the water came from melting ice.

Some kids think it's magic.

Some kids don't know where the water came from.

Water • EMC 862

Investigation 2

Demonstrate a second version of the investigation to clarify students' understanding of condensation.

Materials

- metal pan
- two tall blocks
- metal tray
- ice

Steps to Follow

1. Have a student set the tray on the two blocks so the bottom surface is exposed to air.
2. Have a student set the pan under the tray.
3. Have a third student fill the tray with ice.
   Ask "What do you think will happen?"
4. After several minutes ask "What happened to the tray? Where did the water come from?"

Clarify for students that the melted ice is not leaking through the pan. Remind students that in the evaporation experiment, water turned into a gas and went into the air. Even though they can't see it, water is always in the air. Ask again "Where did the water come from?"

Explain that when the water vapor in the air is cooled, the water changed from a gas back to a liquid. Say "This is called condensation." (Don't expect all students to recall the terms evaporation and condensation.)

Follow up

- Make corrections and additions to the class log. Have students write about the experiment using the logbook form on page 5.

- Reproduce the mini-book *Water in the Air* on pages 44–46 for each student. Read the information together and have students complete the pages.

Extension Activities — Clouds

Explore clouds with your students. Explain that clouds are formed when condensation takes place high in the sky. Read *The Cloud Book* by Tomie de Paola (Scholastic Book Services, 1975) or view a video such as *Clouds (Now I Know Book Video Series)* from Troll. Then do the following experiment.

A Cloud in a Jar

Materials

- jar
- plastic wrap and rubber band
- ice
- water
- small pan
- tongs or oven mitt
- heat source

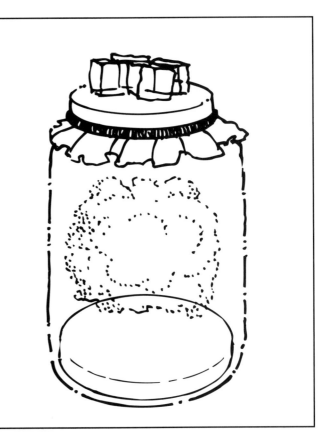

Steps to Follow

1. Fill the jar with boiling water.
2. Pour out all but 1" of the water.
3. Cover the jar with plastic wrap.
4. Place ice on the plastic wrap.
5. Students observe for several minutes. (The inside of the jar will cloud up.)

Follow Up

- Ask "What did you see happen after the ice was put on top of the jar?" *(It became foggy inside.)*
  "Where did the water come from?" *(It condensed from the water vapor in the air inside the jar.)*
  "How is what happened like the way a cloud forms?" *(Clouds are made up of millions of tiny drops formed when water vapor condenses.)*

- Together, write a class log page entitled "Clouds." Using the form on page 5, have students write about the experiment for their individual logs.

Clouds

Clouds are made of tiny water drops.

Rain falls from dark clouds.

Cloud Books

Reproduce pages 47–49 on blue paper for each student to use to make a cloud book.

Materials

- pages 47–49, reproduced for each student
- scissors
- glue
- cotton swabs
- cotton balls
- thin gray paint and paint brush

Steps to Follow

1. Cut the pages apart. (Do not staple together yet.)
2. Make the appropriate cloud on each page following the directions below. Let the glue and paint dry thoroughly before the book is put together. Apply glue to the paper with a cotton swab. Lay the cotton on top of the glue and pat gently.

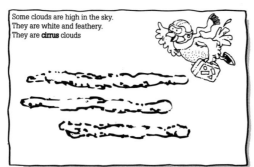

a. Make cirrus clouds on page 1. Pull a cotton ball apart into several pieces. Pull each piece into a thin strip. Put the glue on in long, thin lines. Glue the clouds to the page.

b. Make a cumulus cloud on page 2. Pull a cotton ball to make it light and fluffy. Put glue on the page in the shape of a mountain with a flat bottom. Place the cotton on top of the glue.

c. Make a stratus cloud on page 3. Pull a cotton ball from side-to-side to make a long sheet. Place the cotton on the glue. Paint it with the gray paint.

d. Make fog on page 4. Use crayons to color the picture and add a background. Add the fog with gray paint.

3. Have students write what they have learned about clouds using the logbook form on page 4.
4. Staple the pages together.

Water • EMC 862

Note: Reproduce this form for each student to use with page 39.

Name_____

Water Mystery

Glass 1   Glass 2

Where do you think the water came from?

_____

_____

_____

_____

43

Water in the Air

The hot sun warms the Earth. The heat changes water to **water vapor** (gas). Warm air is lighter than cold air. It goes up into the sky. The water vapor goes up with the warm air.

1

Water vapor is always in the air, but it is invisible. When you breathe out on a cold day, your breath looks like a little cloud. How does this happen?

The water vapor in your warm breath is changed into tiny drops of water when it meets the cold air. This is called **condensation**.

warm day   cold day

1. Water vapor is invisible.	Yes	No
2. You breathe out water vapor.	Yes	No
3. Heat changes water vapor to water.	Yes	No

2

Condensation happens up in the sky, too.

When warm, damp air meets cold air, the water vapor turns into little drops of water. When millions of the little drops come together they make a cloud.

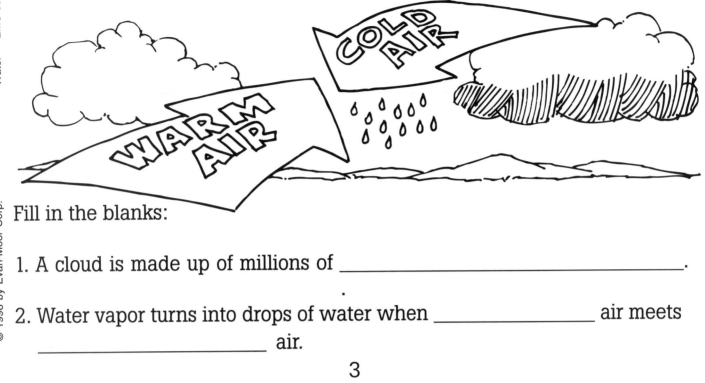

Fill in the blanks:

1. A cloud is made up of millions of _____.

2. Water vapor turns into drops of water when _____ air meets _____ air.

3

- -

You can see water vapor turn into water drops...

when you take a hot bath and the warm air meets the cold mirror.

when you put cold ice cubes in a dry glass and the warm air meets the cold glass.

when the night air becomes cold enough for the water vapor in it to condense. The water drops on the grass are called dew.

4

The color of a cloud lets you know how much water it contains. The darker the cloud, the more water. High, dark clouds cause the biggest rainstorms.

Color these storm clouds.

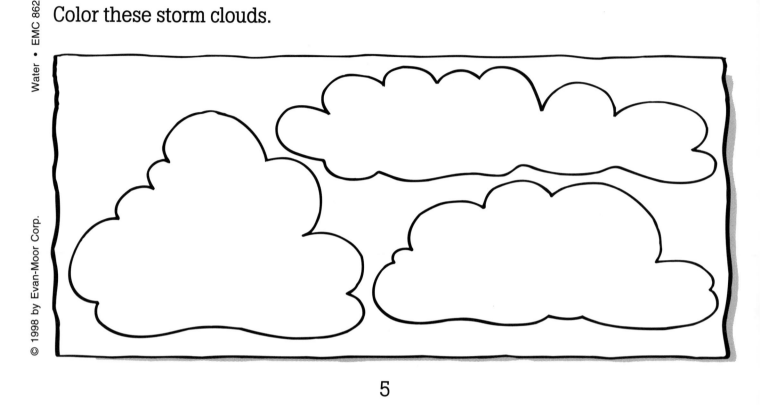

5

Have you ever wanted to walk in a cloud? If you live in a foggy place you already have! Fog is a cloud reaching down close to the ground.

Draw yourself walking in the fog.

Clouds

by

_____

Name

Some clouds are high in the sky.
They are white and feathery.
They are **cirrus** clouds.

Some clouds look like puffy mountains.
They have flat bottoms.
They are **cumulus** clouds.

Some clouds are low in the sky.
They look like gray sheets across the sky.
They are **stratus** clouds.

A cloud that comes down to the ground is called **fog**.

4

Three facts I know about clouds:

1. _____

_____

2. _____

_____

3. _____

_____

5

CONCEPT

The changes water makes are part of a cycle.

Investigating the Rain Cycle

Ask students to draw pictures illustrating some of their experiences with rain. When the pictures are complete, share them with the class as students look for common elements (clouds, falling drops, puddles, etc.). Have students explain how they think rain is made. Write their ideas in the class log on a page entitled "Rain."

Investigate how rain is produced. This can be done in small groups or demonstrated for the whole class.

Materials

- large jar
- sturdy plastic wrap
- rubber band
- water
- black permanent marker

Rain is fun because there are lots of puddles to jump in.

Steps to Follow

1. Fill the jar 1/3 full of water. Mark the water level with black permanent marker.
2. Secure tightly stretched plastic wrap over the top with a rubber band.
3. Ask students to speculate about what will happen.
4. Leave the jar undisturbed for several hours or overnight.
5. Tap lightly on the plastic wrap. Observe what happens. (Drops will fall like rain.)

Follow Up

- Ask students to think about and describe what they observed in the investigation. *(When they looked at the jar, there wasn't as much water as the day before. When they tapped the cover of the jar, drops of water fell to the bottom.)* Then ask students to explain how this is similar to the way rain is made. Help them make the connection by asking questions such as:
     "Why is there less water in the jar?" *(Some of it changed into water vapor. It evaporated.)*
     "Where did the water vapor go?" *(It went to the top of the jar.)*
     "What happened to the water vapor when it touched the plastic wrap?" *(It changed into water drops. It condensed.)*
     "What happened to the water drops when you tapped the plastic wrap?" *(Drops fell to the bottom of the jar.)*
- Explain that the water that condensed on the plastic wrap represents the water that condenses in clouds in the sky.
- Record their ideas in the class log on a page entitled "How Rain is Made." Use copies of page 5 for students to write about how rain is made for their individual logs.

Rain Cycle Information

Check your district audiovisual catalog for a filmstrip or video about the water cycle or read a book such as *Small Cloud* by Ariane (Walker & Co., 1996) or *Rain* by Kay Davis and Wendy Oldfield (Raintree Steck-Vaughn, 1995) to verify what happens in the water cycle.

The Rain Cycle Mini-book

- Reproduce the mini-book on pages 55–57 for each student. Read together and complete pages.

- After reading and discussing the story, have students make any additions or corrections to the class log and their individual logs. (More able students may use the terms evaporation and condensation. You may want to teach the term precipitation to these students.)

- Ask students to help you write a definition of "cycle" for the class logbook. (A cycle is something that happens over and over again in the same way.)

Rain Cycle Sequencing

Materials

- pages 58 and 59, reproduced for each student
- scissors
- glue
- 16" (40.5 cm) square piece of paper

Steps to Follow

1. Students write an explanation of each part of the rain cycle. Depending on the level of your students, you may want to number the pictures in order, talk about what is happening in each, and write a simple sentence on the chalkboard for students to copy.
2. Cut out the pictures and title.
3. Place the title in the center of the large piece of paper.
4. Glue the pictures in a circle to show the cyclical nature of the rain cycle.

Rain Cycle Mural

Make an overhead transparency of page 60 to use as a review of the steps in the rain cycle. Explain to students that they are going to use what they have learned to make a mural about the rain cycle.

The heat of the sun makes water evaporate. The water vapor goes into the air.

Water vapor condenses and makes clouds.

Rain falls from full, dark clouds.

Rain makes streams and rivers. Rivers flow to the sea.

Materials

- long sheet of butcher paper (size will depend on the board on which it will be displayed)
- paint and brushes
- paint shirts or smocks
- newsprint
- newspapers
- writing paper and fine-point marking pen

Steps to Follow

1. Staple the butcher paper to a bulletin board. Divide the paper into four sections.
2. Tape newspapers to the floor under the butcher paper.
3. Divide the class into four groups. Assign one section to each group.
   a. water evaporating up into the air
   b. formation of white, fluffy clouds
   c. rainfall from dark clouds
   d. water flowing back to sea, evaporating into air
4. Students plan their section, deciding who will:
   a. sketch the picture on the newsprint
   b. transfer the sketch to the butcher paper
   c. paint the picture
   d. write a paragraph about what is happening to place under the picture

 Water • EMC 862

Extension Activities

Snow

• Watch a video or read a story about snow. (*Wet Weather: Rain, Showers & Snowflakes* by Jonathan Kohl [Lerner Publications, 1992] is a good book to use.) Students share what they learned about snow. Record their comments in the class log on a page entitled "Snow."

• Compare snow and rain on a Venn diagram.
1. Draw a large Venn diagram on a sheet of butcher paper.
2. Students tell ways snow and rain are alike. Record these on the diagram.
3. Students tell how rain and snow are different. Record this information in the correct boxes.

Snow

Snow falls instead of raindrops when it is very cold.

Snowflakes have six sides.

They are all different.

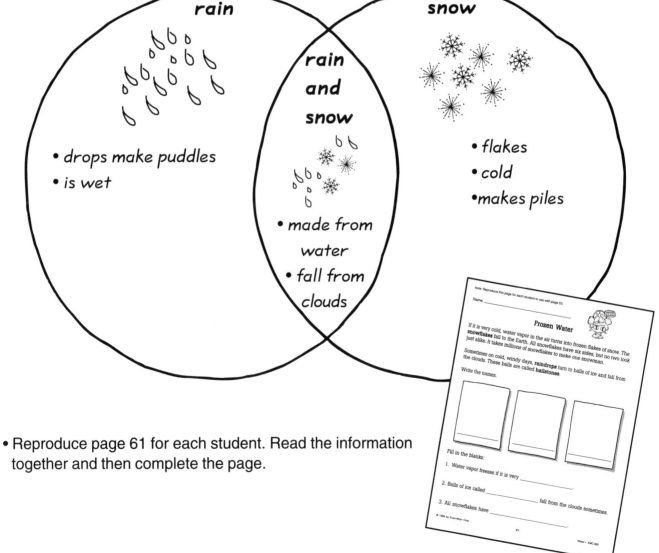

rain

• drops make puddles
• is wet

rain and snow

• made from water
• fall from clouds

snow

• flakes
• cold
• makes piles

Frozen Water

If it is very cold, water vapor in the air turns into frozen flakes of snow. The snowflakes fall to the Earth. All snowflakes have six sides, but no two look just alike. It takes millions of snowflakes to make one snowman.

Sometimes on cold, windy days, **raindrops** turn to balls of ice and fall from the clouds. These balls are called **hailstones**.

Write the names.

Fill in the blanks:

1. Water vapor freezes if it is very _____.

2. Balls of ice called _____ fall from the clouds sometimes.

3. All snowflakes have _____.

• Reproduce page 61 for each student. Read the information together and then complete the page.

     Water • EMC 862

Rainbows

- Have students describe a rainbow. Ask them to name places they have seen rainbows *(in the sky, in the water of a garden sprinkler, on the wall when light hits crystals)*. Read *Raindrops and Rainbows* by Rose Wyler (J. Messner, 1989). Discuss how a rainbow is formed in the sky.

- Have fun making a rainbow.

Materials

- garden hose
- sunlight
- water

Steps to Follow

1. Turn on the garden hose.
2. The person holding the hose stands with his/her back to the sun.
3. Hold the hose so the sunlight goes through the spray.
4. Look for the rainbow to form.

Hold a prism in the sunlight for the same effect. The prism breaks the light into colors just as raindrops do.

Follow up

- Teach students this poem to help them remember how a rainbow is made.
- Reproduce page 62 for each student. Read the paragraph together and then have students complete the page.

When rain falls down
And the sun shines behind,
You can see a rainbow.
It's easy to find.

Sunlight breaks apart
On the raindrops passing by.
Bright colors bend
And an arc fills the sky.

         Water • EMC 862

Rain

- -

There are times when rain falls to the Earth. There are times when the Earth is dry. Both times happen over and over again. They are part of the **rain cycle**.

rainy day

sunny day

The hot sun warms the Earth. The heat causes water to **evaporate** from rivers, lakes, and oceans. Warm air is lighter than cold air. It rises up into the sky. The **water vapor** goes up with the warm air.

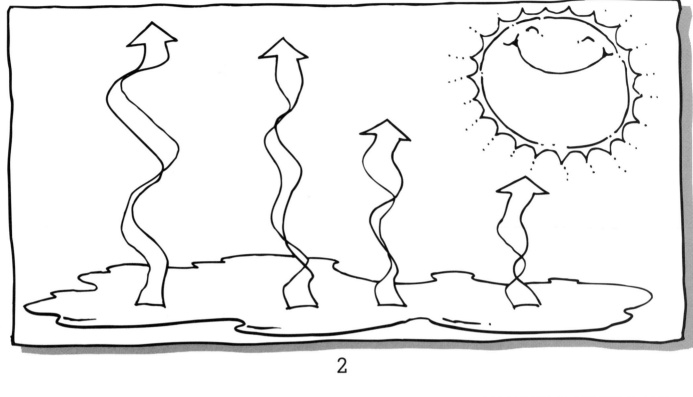

2

As the water vapor rises it meets cold air and **condenses** into drops. Millions of drops come together to make clouds.

Dark clouds contain more water than white clouds.

3

When a cloud gets so full of water it can't hold anymore, water drops begin to fall back to Earth. This is called rain (**precipitation**).

Then the rain cycle starts all over again.

4

Match:

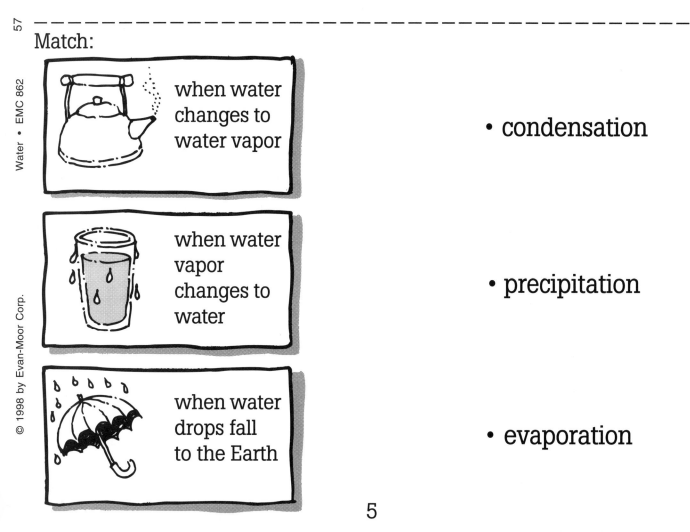

when water changes to water vapor	• condensation
when water vapor changes to water	• precipitation
when water drops fall to the Earth	• evaporation

5

The Rain Cycle

1. Write about each picture.
2. Cut the pictures apart.
3. Paste "The Rain Cycle" in the middle.
4. Paste the other pictures in order around the title.

The Rain Cycle

Name _____

Frozen Water

If it is very cold, water vapor in the air turns into frozen flakes of snow. The **snowflakes** fall to the Earth. All snowflakes have six sides, but no two look just alike. It takes millions of snowflakes to make one snowman.

Sometimes on cold, windy days, **raindrops** turn to balls of ice and fall from the clouds. These balls are called **hailstones**.

Write and draw to show tow kinds of prozen precipitation.

Fill in the blanks:

1. Water vapor freezes if it is very _____.

2. Balls of ice called _____ fall from the clouds sometimes.

3. All snowflakes have _____.

61   Water • EMC 862

Name_____

Rainbows

Sunlight is made up of many colors. We do not see the colors most of the time. When the sunlight meets raindrops, the sunlight breaks up into its different colors. When this happens, we see a rainbow in the sky.

Color the rainbow.

red

orange

yellow

green

blue

indigo

violet

Tell about a time you saw a rainbow.

_____

_____

_____

People need water to live.

We Use Water at Home

- Engage students in a brainstorming session to list all of the ways they used water or saw water being used in their homes before school. Record responses on a class logbook page entitled "We Use Water at Home."

- Pages 66 and 67 are home activity sheets for recording and showing water use. Use one or both pages, depending on the level of your students.

  Give students a chance to name one way they used water at home. After going around the class two or three times, ask about things they might have left out.

  "Does anyone have _____ on their list?" *(water for houseplants, washing clothes, flushing the toilet, washing windows, etc.)*

  Add new items mentioned to the list in the class log.

- Build categories of the items listed in the class log. Ask students to decide on three things that could go together. List these on the chalkboard and think of a name for the category. For example, wash dishes, take a bath, and brush teeth could go together in a category called "for cleaning." Ask "Does anything else on our list go in this category?"

  Repeat to create other categories of water use (cooking; drinking water; making things).

We Use Water at Home

drank a glass of water

put water in fish tank

took a bath

washed clothes

mom washed the dishes in water

filled dog's water dish

watered the grass

used water to brush teeth

dad put water in the coffee pot

cooked oatmeal in water

Workers Use Water at School

Have groups of students observe or interview school personnel to find out how they use water.

1. Set up visits in advance so workers are prepared to tell and show how they use water in their jobs.
2. Prepare questions to ask. Record responses on paper or video tape. (Younger students will need adult help.)
3. Share what is learned in the interviews. Show the video tape if one has been made.
4. Record information on a class log page entitled "People Use Water at School." Have students write in their individual logs using the form on page 4.

Earth — The Water Planet

Reproduce the mini-book on pages 68–69 for each student. Read the book together. Have students complete the pages.

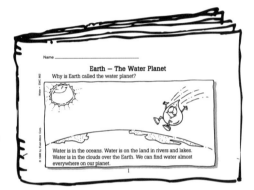

We Use Water

Make a class book about how people use water.

Materials

- two 9" x 12" (23 x 30.5 cm) sheets of colored construction paper
- 9" x 12" (23 x 30.5 cm) drawing paper
- crayons or marking pens
- pencil

Steps to Follow

1. Select a student to do a cover illustration for the book.
2. Each student chooses a water use from the class log to illustrate and write about.
3. Staple the pages together with the cover.

Extension Activities

Making Water Pure

- Read pages 20 to 37 of *The Magic School Bus at the Waterworks* by Joanna Cole (Scholastic, 1986) for an explanation of how cities make sure water is clean.
- Do the water filtering demonstration on this page.
- Make an overhead transparency of page 70. Go through each step of the purification process with students. Then give each student a copy of page 71 and have them move through the maze from the reservoir to the house.
- Visit your local water purification plant. Record what they learn in the class log on a page entitled "Pure Water."

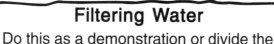

Filtering Water

Do this as a demonstration or divide the class into small groups.

Materials

- tall bottle or jar
- funnel
- sand
- small gravel
- dirty water

Steps to Follow

1. Set the funnel in the mouth of the bottle.
2. Fill the funnel with sand and gravel in layers — gravel, sand, gravel, sand.
3. Pour the dirty water into the funnel.
4. Observe the water as it drains into the bottle.
5. Discuss what happened to "clean up" the dirty water.

Using Water Wisely

- Engage students in a discussion about water usage. Explain that in many places around the world there is not enough fresh water for people and their animals and crops. Ask "Can you think of ways people waste water? Can you think of ways to use water wisely?" Record their ideas on the chalkboard in two lists — Wasting Water, Saving Water.
- Reproduce page 72 for each student. They are to mark wise and wasteful uses of water.

Wasting Water	Saving Water
• let water run when you aren't using it	• turn off the water while you brush your teeth
• wash the sidewalk with water	• only take as much water as you need
• take a drink of water and throw most of it away	• sweep up leaves on the sidewalk

Water • EMC 862

The _____ Family Uses Water

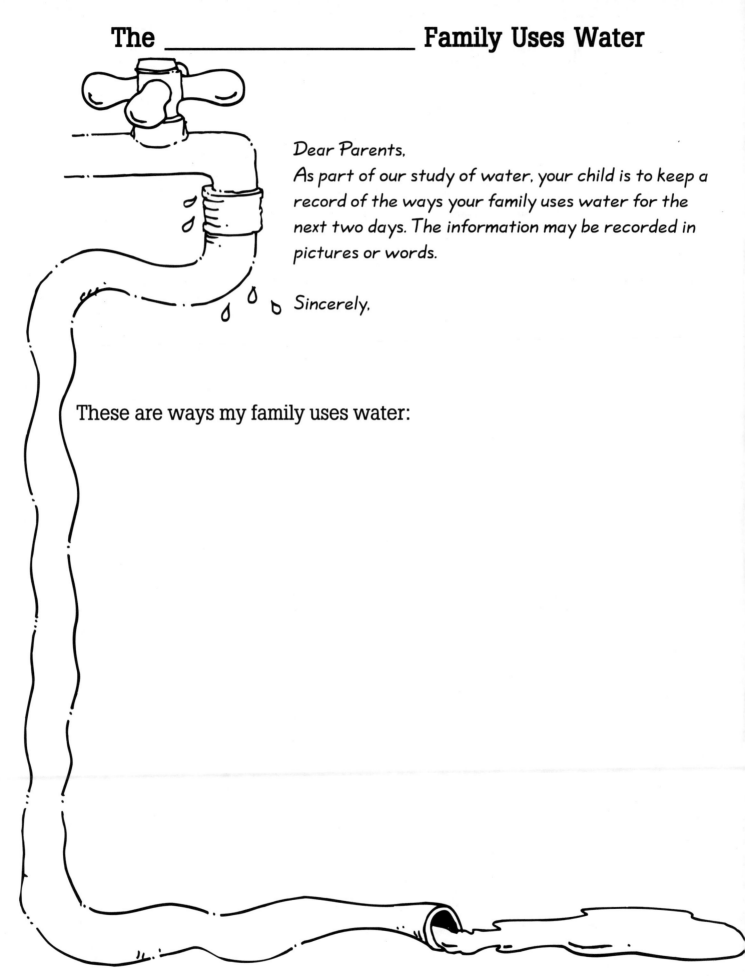

Dear Parents,
As part of our study of water, your child is to keep a record of the ways your family uses water for the next two days. The information may be recorded in pictures or words.

Sincerely,

These are ways my family uses water:

Water • EMC 862

Name _____

Where We Use Water at Home

Mark an X on the places you find water in and around a house.

Water • EMC 862

Earth — The Water Planet

Why is Earth called the water planet?

Water is in the oceans. Water is on the land in rivers and lakes. Water is in the clouds over the Earth. We can find water almost everywhere on our planet.

1

Color the water blue.
Color the land green.

2

Why is water important?

Plants, animals, and people all need water to live. Plants use water to grow and to make food. Animals and people drink water to grow and be healthy.

People need water every day. We cannot live very long without water.

3

Plants and animals need different amounts of water.

    Put an X on things that need a lot of water.

    Make a box around things that need a little water.

cactus

desert tortoise

flowers

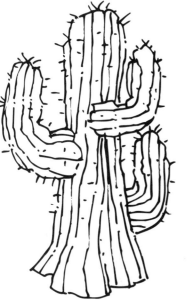

fish

houseplant

4

Note: Make an overhead transparency of this purification plant to use with page 65.

Water Purification

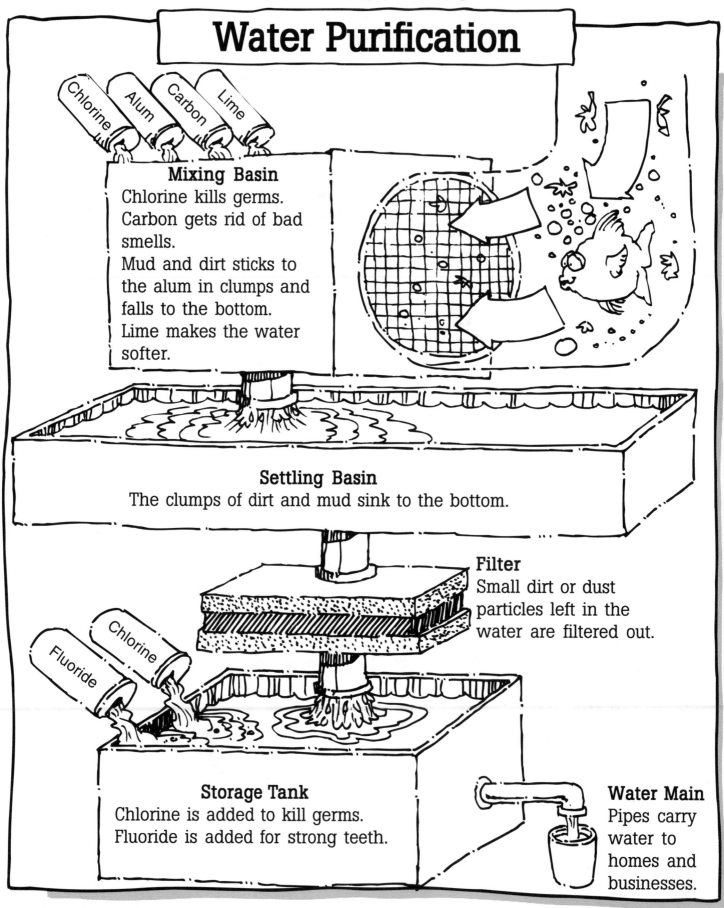

Mixing Basin
Chlorine kills germs.
Carbon gets rid of bad smells.
Mud and dirt sticks to the alum in clumps and falls to the bottom.
Lime makes the water softer.

Settling Basin
The clumps of dirt and mud sink to the bottom.

Filter
Small dirt or dust particles left in the water are filtered out.

Storage Tank
Chlorine is added to kill germs.
Fluoride is added for strong teeth.

Water Main
Pipes carry water to homes and businesses.

Water • EMC 862

Name _____

How Does Water Get to Your House?

Move through the maze from the reservoir to your house.

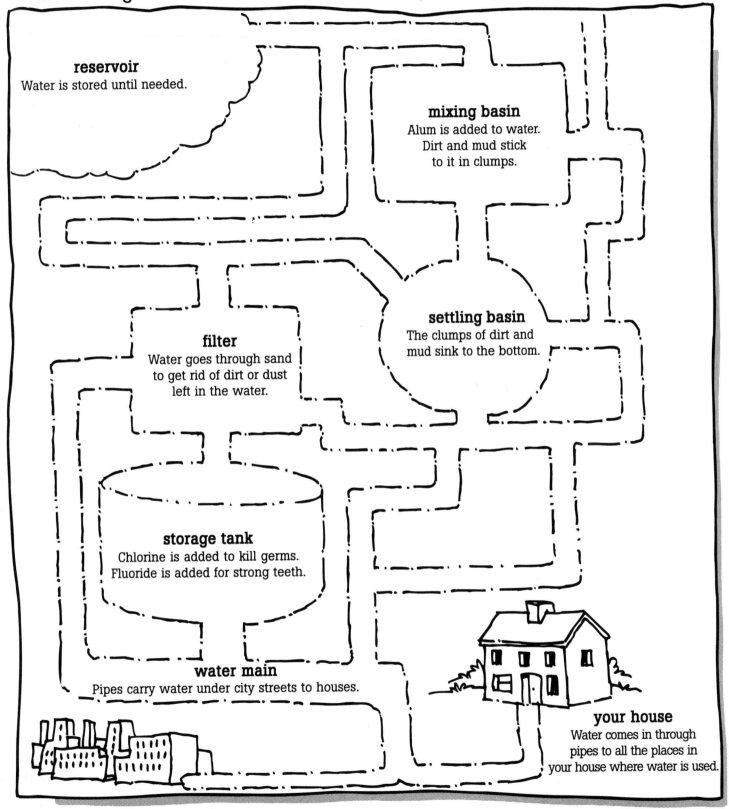

reservoir
Water is stored until needed.

mixing basin
Alum is added to water.
Dirt and mud stick
to it in clumps.

filter
Water goes through sand
to get rid of dirt or dust
left in the water.

settling basin
The clumps of dirt and
mud sink to the bottom.

storage tank
Chlorine is added to kill germs.
Fluoride is added for strong teeth.

water main
Pipes carry water under city streets to houses.

your house
Water comes in through
pipes to all the places in
your house where water is used.

Water • EMC 862

Name _____

We Use Water

Mark the correct face.   😞 wasteful 😊 wise

72   Water • EMC 862

Moving water can do work.

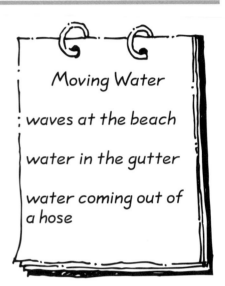

When Water Moves

- Pour water from a pitcher into a glass. Ask students to describe what the water is doing as it goes from the pitcher to the glass (moving). Challenge them to think of places they have seen water moving. You may need to use questions to help them move beyond "out of the faucet into the sink" types of answers.

  Point to each place in the list and ask "What happened when the water moved?"

  waves at beach — moved sand, brought shells to shore
  in gutter — moved twigs and dirt along
  out of hose — watered the grass

- Record information on a class log page entitled "Moving Water."

- Tell students that they are going to learn more about moving water by doing an experiment (page 74).

Moving Water

waves at the beach

water in the gutter

water coming out of a hose

Water • EMC 862

Water Wheel Experiment

Students make water wheels to explore how water can do work.

Divide students into small groups. Have each student in the group make a water wheel and then do the exploration together.

Materials

- page 76, reproduced on tagboard for each student
- plastic dishpan for water or access to a faucet
- water
- pencil
- scissors

Steps to Follow

1. Set up an experiment area. Either fill the dishpan half full of water and provide a pitcher of water or have students work at a sink half full of water.
2. Cut out the wheel, cut along all lines, and fold each section over to form a "flap" to catch the water.
3. Push the wheel onto a pencil (younger students may need help with this step). Wiggle the wheel until it moves freely around the pencil.
4. Students in a group take turns holding their water wheels half in and half out of the water to see if they turn. They then take turns pouring water against the wheel (or holding it under the faucet) to see if it will turn.
5. Students record what they observe in their individual logs, using the form on page 5.

Follow up

- After everyone has had a chance to try their wheels, select several students to share what they observed. Students should come to the conclusion that water must be moving in order to do work. Record their discoveries in the class log on a page entitled "Can Water Do Work?"

Can Water Do Work?

Water can do work if it is moving.

Moving water made our water wheels turn.

- Reinforce the idea that water must move to do work. Make an overhead transparency of the water wheel and the grinding stone on page 77. Explain that water wheels such as these were used in the past to grind grain into flour. Have students identify the two wheels and explain what would make them move. *(The stream moving past the mill would cause the water wheel to turn. This would turn the shaft leading to the grinding stone, which would then turn, crushing the grain.)*

Water • EMC 862

Hydroelectricity

- Explain that we use moving water today to make some of the electricity we use. Read a book such as *Rain to Dams* by Clint Twist (Glouster Press, 1990) or appropriate sections of *Water Energy* by Graham Rickard (Gareth Stevens Children's Books, 1991) to introduce hydroelectricity.

- Make an overhead transparency of page 78 to use with students as you review the flow of water through the hydroelectric plant.

---

1 Water from the dam's reservoir falls through the floodgates.

2 The water gathers speed as it flows down the tunnel.

3 The turbine is spun by the moving water.

4 As the turbine turns, it spins magnets in the generator. This makes electricity in the coils that are around the magnets. The electricity is carried away in cables.

5 Water flows out of the turbine into a tunnel that carries the water back to the river.

- Reproduce the mini-book on pages 79–80 for each student. Read the text together.

- Check your district audiovisual catalog for a film or video about hydroelectricity.

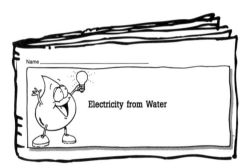

Name _____

Electricity from Water

- Visit a dam or hydroelectric plant.

Water Wheel

1. Cut all dotted lines.

2. Fold.

3. Put on a pencil.

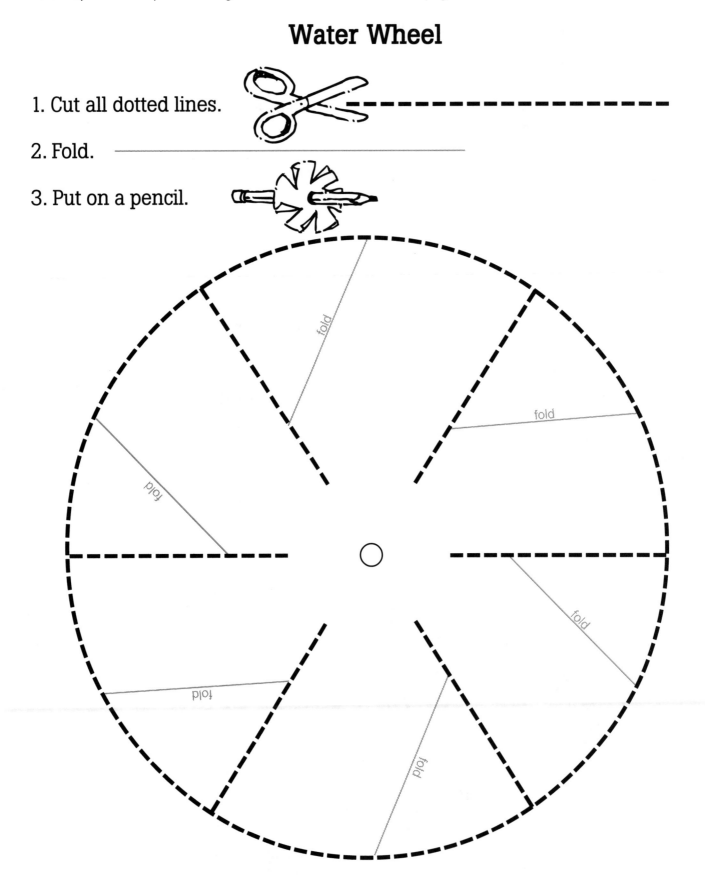

Water Does Work

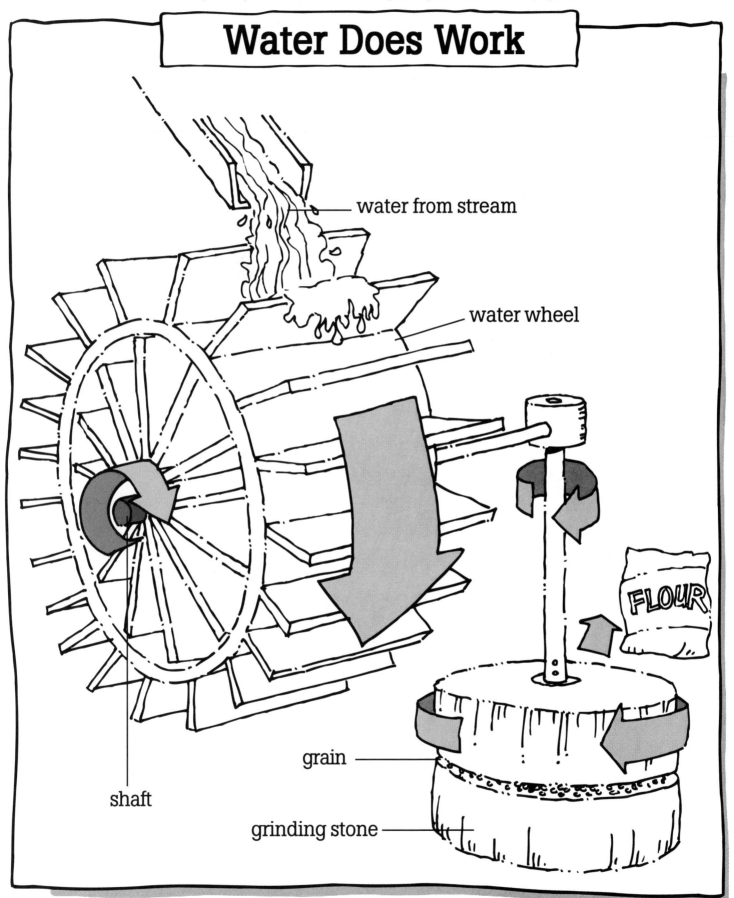

water from stream

water wheel

FLOUR

shaft

grain

grinding stone

Hydroelectric Plant

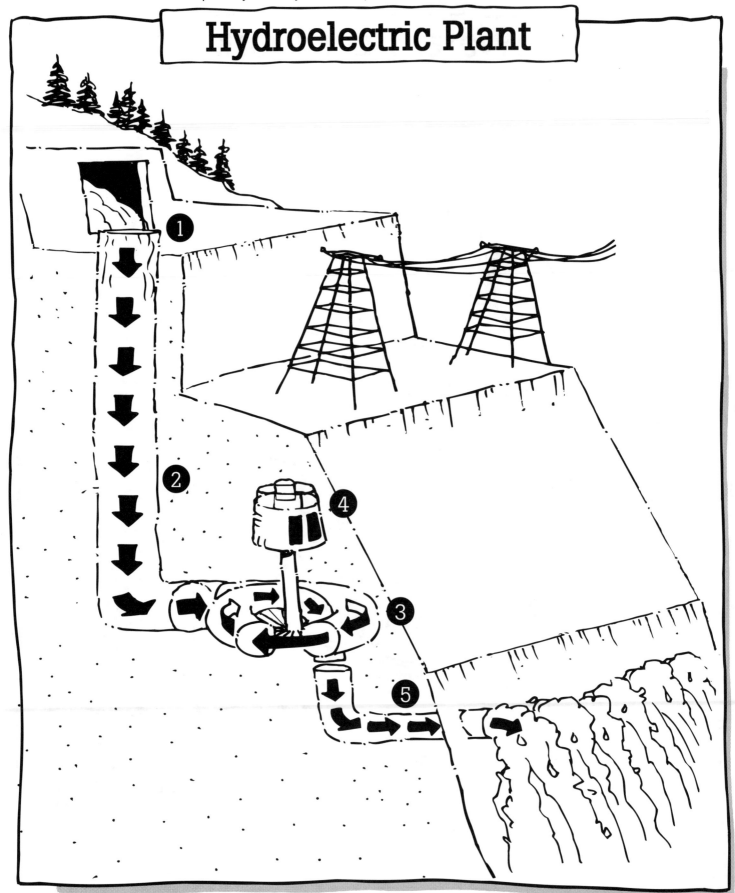

Name _____

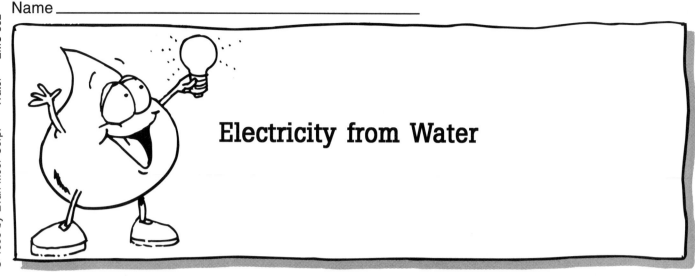

Electricity from Water

Falling water provides the power for hydroelectric plants to make electricity. The water can come from a waterfall or from a reservoir. A dam holds back water from a river to create a reservoir.

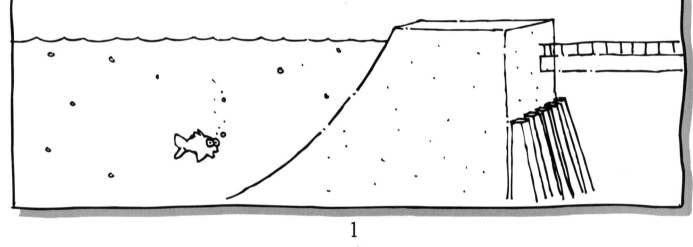

1

The dam has a floodgate that can be raised or lowered. When the floodgate is open, water can flow through a tunnel. The water goes through tunnels to the turbines.

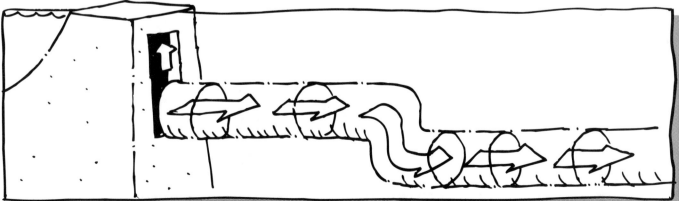

2

The tunnel gets narrower as it gets closer to the turbine. This makes the water move even faster.

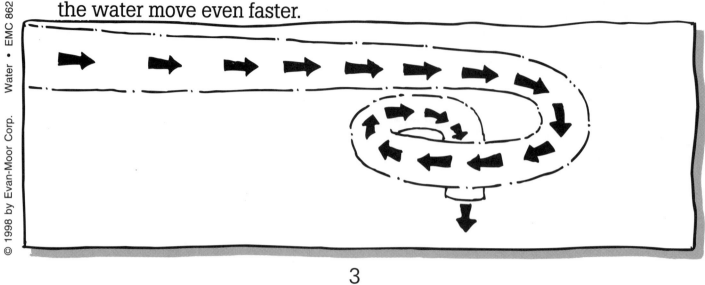

3

The turbine is spun by the water. As the turbine turns, it spins magnets in the generator. This makes electricity in wire coils that are around the magnets. The electricity is carried away in cables.

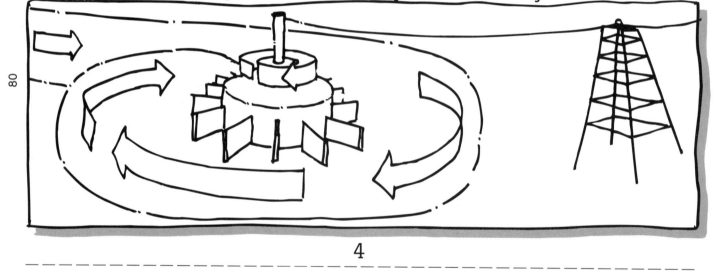

4

The water flows out of the turbine and back into the river.

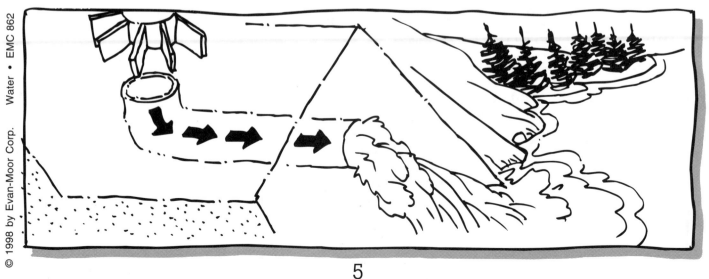

5